CONTENTS

Author and artist:
Mark Bergin studied at Eastbourne College of Art and has specialized in historical reconstructions, aviation and maritime subjects for over 20 years. He lives in Bexhill-on-Sea with his wife and three children.

Historical consultant:
Andrew Robertshaw taught history before joining the National Army Museum, Chelsea, in 1984. He is currently responsible for the Museum's education services. He is also an author, military historian and battlefield guide. He lives in Surrey with his wife and daughter.

Additional artists: **Gerald Wood, Ray and Corinne Burrows, Tony Townsend, John James**

Series creator and designer: **David Salariya**
Editor: **Karen Barker Smith**
Assistant Editor: **Michael Ford**

U.S. Editors: **Joanna Callihan** and **Lindsay Mizer**

Children's Publishing

This edition published in the United States of America in 2003 by Peter Bedrick Books an imprint of McGraw-Hill Children's Publishing A Division of The McGraw-Hill Companies 8787 Orion Place Columbus, OH 43240-4027

www.MHkids.com

Library of Congress data is on file with McGraw-Hill Children's Publishing

Created, designed and produced by The Salariya Book Company Ltd 25 Marlborough Place, Brighton BN1 1UB

Please visit the Salariya Book Company at: www.salariya.com
www.book-house.co.uk

ISBN 1-57768-593-8

Printed and bound in Belgium.
Printed on paper from sustainable forests.

Photographic credits
t=top b=bottom c=center l=left r=right

The Art Archive/ Belvoir Castle/ Eileen Tweedy: 34/35t
The Art Archive/ Eileen Tweedy: 18/19, 34b
The Art Archive/ JFB: 17r
The Art Archive/ Harper Collins Publishers: 30
The Art Archive/ Musée des Beaux Art Nantes/ Dagli Orti: 20 bl
The Art Archive/ Musée du Château de Versailles/ Dagli Orti: 28bl
The Art Archive/ National Archives Washington DC: 38tr, 39c
The Art Archive/ Wellington Museum, London/ Eileen Tweedy: 31tl
Ashmolean Museum, Oxford, UK/ The Bridgeman Art Library: 15br
Breslich and Foss: 22r, 23l, 33l, 36l, 37r, 41l
Bridgeman Art Library: 12/13, 25tl
Cheltenham Art Gallery and Museum, Gloucestershire, UK/ The Giraudon/ The Bridgeman Art Library: 25tr
Kunsthistorisches Museum, Vienna, Austria/ The Bridgeman Art Library: 10tl
Mountain High Maps/ copyright 1993 Digital Wisdom Inc: 6/7c, 8tl, 10r, 12tl, 13tl, 16tl, 18tr, 20tl, 22tr, 26tl, 30tr, 36tl
Nigel Hillyard of The Sealed Knot: 14l, 15tl
Smith Art Gallery and Museum, Stirling, Scotland/ The Bridgeman Art Library: 19tr
Victoria and Albert Museum, London, UK/ The Bridgeman Art Library: 21tl

©The Salariya Book Company: 1, 2/3, 5, 9, 11br, 13t, 19tl, 22bc, 27tr, 27l, 29r, 31tr, 31r, 35bl, 37cl, 37b, 40tr, 41bl, 46/47, 48

Every effort has been made to trace copyright holders. The Salariya Book Company apologises for any unintentional omissions and would be pleased, in such cases, to add an acknowledgement in future editions.

BATTLE ZONES

Warfare in the 16th to 19th Centuries

Written and illustrated by
Mark Bergin

PETER BEDRICK BOOKS

Columbus, Ohio

OVERVIEW

Between the 16th and 19th centuries many conflicts were fought around the globe. These were partly due to the ideologies and expansionist policies of countries and their rulers. Over this period, military strategies and fighting techniques changed dramatically with the use of new weapons, such as gunpowder. By mobilizing strong armies and navies to control more of the world's surface, European powers planned to build vast empires in the 16th and 17th centuries. Many of the wars in the following period saw those empires crumble as occupied territories tried to fight back.

ARMADA, 1588
In 1588, King Philip II of Spain sent a large invasion fleet to attack Elizabeth I's England. This was successfully fought off by a smaller fleet led by Sir Francis Drake.

REVOLUTIONARY WAR
Although Britain's armed forces were among the best in the world, the American colonies rebelled against them in 1775 to claim their freedom. They were helped by Britain's old enemies, the French and Spanish.

NORTH AMERICA

EUROPE

Atlantic Ocean

AFRICA

Pacific Ocean

SOUTH AMERICA

U.S. CIVIL WAR
The American Civil War (1861-1865) was one of the most significant events in the history of the United States. Three million soldiers fought on both sides in the conflict. Northern (Union) states and southern (Confederate) states fought each other over whether the national government or the individual states should have more power.

INDIAN WARS
North American Indians fought many battles with the new settlers who colonized their land. The new settlers brought diseases, put up boundaries on native hunting grounds, and slaughtered buffalo herds. By the 1860s, the U.S. government moved many tribes to reservations, but many chose to fight against such oppression.

ENGLISH CIVIL WAR

King Charles I and Parliament fought over the power to govern the country between 1642 and 1643. The country was divided in its support for either side.

JACOBITE REBELLION

In 1745, an uprising was led in Scotland by Prince Charles Stuart. He sailed from France and united various clan leaders to take the crown of England from King George II.

FREDERICK THE GREAT

Frederick (ruled 1740-1786) was king of Prussia (present-day northern Germany). He increased Prussia's territory and influence by campaigning against his neighbors in the Seven Years' War.

RUSSIA

JAPAN

CRIMEAN WAR

The Crimean War was caused by a dispute between Russia, France, and the Ottoman Empire. They fought over the rights of protection of Christian shrines in the Ottoman-controlled holy land.

SAMURAI WARLORDS

The samurai were the military elite of Japan, similar to the medieval knights of Europe. Their military power and political skills enabled them to control local governments and lands. Samurai clans were in a continual state of civil war until 1603, when they all came under the ruling dynasty of Tokugawa Ieyasu.

NAPOLEONIC WARS

Napoleon was one of the greatest commanders in history. He changed the borders in Europe between 1799 and 1815. This French general had ambitious plans to conquer all of Europe and then Russia as well. This led to a 15-year period of turmoil and battles around Europe, from Spain to Russia.

Mounted samurai warriors ride out from Himeji Castle (below)

SAMURAI CASTLES
Samurai castles were situated to guard the routes connecting the *daimyo* (warlord) territories with hostile neighboring lands. If a site lacked strong natural defenses, artificial barriers, such as moats and walls, were built. Between 1570 and 1690, the golden age of Japanese castle construction occurred.

SHOGUNS AND SAMURAI

The samurai were the warrior class who served local lords in medieval Japan. Military families had dominated Japan from around the 12th century, after the emperor had been replaced by a military overlord, called a *shogun*. Many years of turmoil followed, with continual outbreaks of fighting between rival lords. Throughout these years of unrest, the samurai followed the code of *bushido* (the way of the warrior). The basis of this code was an unquestioning loyalty to one's lord. This bond of service was often so strong that if a lord died in battle, his followers might commit mass suicide rather than surrender or serve another lord.

The Battle of Sekigahara, on October 21st, 1600, was the most decisive in the history of Japan. Ishida Mitsunari (with 100,000 troops) and Tokugawa Ieyasu (with 75,000 troops) fought to be master of Japan. After a fierce hand-to-hand battle, 30,000 men lay dead. Ieyasu won and was given the title of Shogun three years later.

HIMEJI CASTLE
The castle (above and below) was completed in 1609. This beautiful structure was covered in intricately carved and painted woodwork. Other features included multiple gateways, courtyards, reception halls, watchtowers, stables, and workshops.

a b c d e f g

TYPES OF SAMURAI WARRIORS

a. An archer's "kyudo" bamboo bow could be shot from horseback or standing.

b. An *arquebusier* was a samurai with a type of musket.

c. A spearman carried spears up to 5 yards long.

d. A standard-bearer.

e. An army commander wore full metal armor and a *kabuto* (crested helmet).

f. Bodyguard with a *daito* (long sword).

g. Low-class *bushi* (foot soldier) armed with a *nagamaki* (a kind of slashing spear with a long wooden handle and a sword-like blade).

ARMOR

Elaborate samurai armor (below) was made from lacquered iron and leather segments held together with silk cords. The sleeves and legs were made from chain mail, and helmets often had crests and iron face masks. Attached to their backs were colorful banners with their clan's crests on them.

Head detail from a samurai suit of armor

A 16th-century portrait of Sir Francis Drake

ARMADA, 1588

Philip II of Spain had plenty of reasons to go to war with England. English privateers were raiding Spanish ports and ships, and Queen Elizabeth I's government was persecuting Catholics in England. Philip's plan was for two forces to link up, cross the channel, and attack—from Spain the Duke of Medina Sidonia's fleet, and from the Spanish Netherlands the Duke of Parma's army. The Armada of 130 ships and 19,000 troops set sail on May 28th, 1588, from Lisbon. After some minor skirmishes at sea, the Spanish anchored off Calais and were attacked at night by English fireships. Scattered, the Armada was considerably damaged in a nine-hour battle between Gravelines (France) and Ostend (in what is now Belgium). A strong south-westerly wind drove the remaining ships into the North Sea, and Spanish commanders ordered them to return home by routing north of Scotland and the Irish Sea.

Sir Francis Drake (above) was one of the most feared captains at sea. He had sailed around the world in his ship the *Golden Hinde* (1577-1580) looking for treasure. In 1587, Drake led a force of 25 ships and made a series of devastating attacks against Spanish ports.

Map showing the route taken by the Spanish Armada (right)

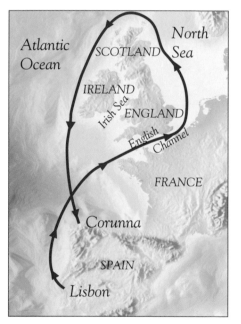

In the initial battles with the Armada, the English were so far out of range that their cannon did little damage. But after the Battle of Plymouth, the Spanish ship *San Salvador* blew up, and the *Rosario* was captured by Drake after losing a mast.

Drake looks at the Spanish fleet from the deck of an English galleon (left)

ARK ROYAL
English ships fought at long range with their guns, whereas the Spanish ships were designed to fight traditionally, closing in on and boarding with masses of soldiers. The English flagship was the *Ark Royal* (left), built in 1587. The gun ports were placed below decks but well above the water-line. The ship had 24 gunners, 150 sailors, and 76 soldiers on board.

SPANISH SHIPS
The Armada flagship was the Portuguese galleon *San Martin* (below), with 48 guns. Other Armada ships were galleasses (with sails and oars) and galleys (with oars only). Galleasses were slow but heavily armed. Just after the Armada set sail, rough seas forced the fleet's four galleys to turn back.

Ark Royal

Spanish ship wrecked by storms

THE WEATHER TAKES ITS TOLL
Storms lashed the Armada on its route around Scotland and Ireland. Many ships were lost along the coast, forced ashore and smashed on the rocks (above). The leader of the Armada, Medina Sidonia, got his flagship back to Spain on September 21st. Around 15,000 men never returned, and less than half the ships made it into port.

A "morion" helmet as worn by Spanish soldiers in the Armada

ENGLISH CIVIL WAR

England

Conflict arose between Charles I of England and Parliament over how to deal with Scotland and Ireland. The king was causing religious unrest in both of these countries by enforcing Protestant rule. Charles needed money from taxes to do this, but Parliament refused to help him. They demanded that he dismiss some of his senior aides, whom they distrusted. When Charles attempted to arrest five troublesome members of Parliament on January 4th, 1642, he angered many people and riots broke out in London. The king was forced to flee the city. By October, the king had raised an army of 13,000 men, and they headed toward London. Under the leadership of the earl of Essex, the Parliamentary troops left the capital to cut him off. The forces first met at Edgehill (October 23rd). The king narrowly won this battle but later retreated to establish headquarters in Oxford. Although the Royalists had success in much of England, especially in the southwest (capturing Bristol on July 26th, 1643), Charles still did not advance on London.

A "mortuary hilt" sword, as used by cavalry soldiers during the Civil War

MAJOR BATTLES

The map above shows the principal battles between the Royalists (Cavaliers) and the Parliamentarians (Roundheads).

A 19th-century painting of the Battle of Marston Moor, 1644 (below)

MARSTON MOOR, JULY 2ND, 1644

Under Leslie, first earl of Leven, the Scots came south and joined with the Parliamentary forces. At the Battle of Marston Moor (below), near York, these forces crushed the Royalists, led by Prince Rupert (the king's nephew and duke of Newcastle). York now surrendered to the Parliamentarian army and the Scots stormed Newcastle on October 19th, with 21,000 men.

NEW MODEL ARMY

In the winter of 1644-1645, the British Parliament suffered heavy defeats and was having problems with its army regarding salary disputes. The solution was to bring together old army units under the leadership of commanders Sir Thomas Fairfax and Oliver Cromwell. This was known as the "New Model Army," consisting of 22,000 full-time paid and trained men. This army met and defeated the Royalists at Naseby on June 14th, 1645, and by May of 1646, the king was under siege at Oxford. The Civil War officially ended when Oxford surrendered to Parliament on June 24th, but the king escaped from the city in disguise and gave himself up to the Scots. At first, the Scots would not help Charles, because he would not agree to their demands. Having again escaped Cromwell's clutches, Charles eventually persuaded the Scots to help him, but their army was defeated by Cromwell and Fairfax at the Battle of Preston in 1648. The king was taken under arrest to Windsor, and after a vote in Parliament, King Charles was made to stand trial as a traitor to his country. He was sentenced to death and executed by having his head cut off.

ARTILLERY
The heavy artillery of an army was stationed at the rear, where it could fire over the heads of the infantry.

Smaller cannons (left), that fired nails and scrap iron in canvas bags, were positioned in front of the infantry.

Reconstruction of a small cannon used in the English Civil War

Helmet

Leather tunic

Short-barreled musket

Roundheads wore red sashes early in the war to identify themselves in battle

CAVALRYMEN
These soldiers carried a sword and a short-barreled musket. The main strategy was to advance at a quick trot until in range of the enemy. The men in the front fired, then wheeled away. In their second charge, they advanced at a gallop using their swords.

THE DEATH OF A KING
After a week-long trial, King Charles I was executed on January 30th, 1649 (above). Before his head was cut off, his final words were, "I am a martyr to the people." Oliver Cromwell had signed the King's death warrant himself.

Reconstruction of pikemen from the English Civil War

PIKEMEN
Pikemen (above) were foot soldiers armed with 16-foot-long pointed pikes. They stood at the center of battle formations to keep advancing enemy cavalry at bay. Well-disciplined pikemen, brave enough to hold their ground, could do tremendous damage to cavalry charging straight at them.

Death mask of Oliver Cromwell (right), made by taking a wax impression of his face at the time of his death

TYRANT OR SAVIOR?
After the execution of Charles I, Oliver Cromwell brutally suppressed uprisings in both Scotland and Ireland. A new Parliament was formed, consisting of 140 "godly" (religious) men who made Cromwell "Lord Protector" (temporary Head of State). His first act was to make a peace treaty with the Dutch in 1654, which ended years of trade wars and helped the British Empire expand overseas.

WAR OF THE SPANISH SUCCESSION, 1701-1714

At the end of the 17th century, the king of Spain, Charles II, died without an heir. All of Europe fought for the vast territories owned by the Hapsburg family, which included large parts of Europe and lands in the Americas. It soon became a struggle between the two most powerful families in Europe, the Hapsburgs under Leopold I and the Bourbons under Louis XIV. Fearing that one nation might become too powerful, the British and their Dutch allies sided with Leopold I to stop the French from becoming a European superpower.

JOHN CHURCHILL, DUKE OF MARLBOROUGH
During the war, English commander Marlborough (right) waged ten successful campaigns, besieged over thirty towns, and never lost a battle or contest.

Duke of Marlborough

CHAIN OF COMMAND
Marlborough's army was well organized. He relayed messages through "aides-de-camp" (below), foot-runners who acted as his eyes and ears on the battlefield.

Aide-de-camp

16

Long coat

Sword

In 1702 the Duke of Marlborough marched to join forces with Prince Eugene of Savoy to bar the way of the French advancing on Vienna in Austria. The armies fought near the Bavarian village of Blenheim in August 1704, where the French and Bavarian forces lost around 30,000 men. Later in the war, in 1708, Marlborough scored a decisive victory over the French Duke of Vendome at the battle of Oudenarde. Following this, the war was brought to a conclusion as the British and Dutch forces overwhelmed their enemies over the next few years.

The French army of Louis XIV (above) had long coats, waistcoats, breeches and stockings. Each carried a sword and flintlock musket with a bayonet. Sergeants wore cuffs edged with gold lace.

DRAGONS
DE MONSEIGNEUR LE DUC
DE PENTHIEVRE,
En Garnison à Quimper, en Bretagne.

PROPAGANDA
Recruiting poster (above) for the dragoons of the Duke of Vendome, who was also known as the Duke of Penthievre. Dragoons were heavily armed cavalry troops.

Flintlock musket with bayonet

Cannon

Drum

17

JACOBITE REBELLION

*I*n 1708, the unpopular English king, James II, had been replaced on the throne by his daughter, Mary, and her husband, William. After a failed uprising in 1715, James fled to France. A generation later the Jacobites (as supporters of James were called) were led by his grandson Charles Stuart, or 'Bonnie Prince Charlie'. Charles hoped for support from the French, who were at war with the English king, George II. A small invasion force set sail from France in July 1745, but was intercepted by the Royal Navy. The Prince's ship escaped and he landed in Scotland and began to drum up support from the Highland clans. By September they had captured Edinburgh with 2,500 men.

Charles's force marched over the border into England and took control of Carlisle after a six-day siege. The force now advanced towards London but, discouraged by lack of French support, the Highland chiefs forced Charles to turn back on 6th December. The final battle of the uprising was at Culloden on 16th April, 1746. A larger British force under the command of the Duke of Cumberland dealt a decisive blow and shattered the rebel army.

Great Britain

Duke of Cumberland

CULLODEN
As Charles deserted the battlefield at Culloden, Cumberland (right) ordered his soldiers to show no mercy to the Highlanders. They were slaughtered in retreat and Cumberland became known as 'the Butcher'.

HIGHLANDER'S SWORD
The basket-hilt broadsword (left) would have been used at Culloden. The full sword is almost a metre long. The hilt was designed to encase the user's hand, protecting it from enemy blows.

BONNIE PRINCE CHARLIE
Charles Stuart (above) was 25 years old at the time of the rebellion. He escaped and married in 1772, but had no children. He was the last Stuart to fight for the British throne.

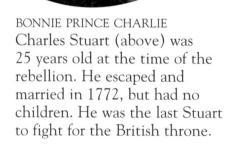

Mitre-style hat

Musket

Match case

GRENADIER
On the left is a typical English soldier of the 1745 period. The royal crown and white horse of Hanover is seen on his mitre-style hat. He has two pouches: one for grenades and another to carry cartridges. He also has a brass match case fixed above the buckle to store matches to light the grenades. He wears long marching gaiters.

Marching gaiters

FREDERICK THE GREAT

Frederick the Great of Prussia (part of present-day Germany and Poland) had a well-trained army and used it to great effect when he invaded the Austrian-ruled land of Silesia (part of present-day Poland) on 16th December, 1740. The Austrians, weakened by a recent war with the Ottomans, were not expecting the attack and the province quickly fell.

In 1741 Frederick invaded Bohemia (in the present-day Czech Republic), capturing Prague after a short siege. In 1745 the Austrians, under Charles of Lorraine, were determined to drive the

Musket with bayonet

Prussians from Silesia, but were out-manoeuvred by Frederick's well-drilled infantry and cavalry. These victories forced the Austrians to accept the Prussian claim to Silesia at the Peace of Dresden. With the rise of Prussia, Russia and Austria allied themselves to crush their expanding enemy and between 1756 and 1763 most of Europe was at war. The French sided with Russia and Austria, while British, Swedish and German rulers allied themselves with Frederick. Finally, in 1762, a Russo-Prussian peace was ordered by Peter III of Russia and hostilities ceased. The Austrians followed suit on 15th February, 1763.

A GREAT LEADER
Frederick II (left) spent his childhood in rigorous military training and education. As an adult he studied music and French literature. He directed the internal affairs of his country with passion and prudence. By the time he died he had nearly doubled the area of the Prussian kingdom.

PRUSSIAN INFANTRY
Frederick the Great's army was well paid and well equipped. It had grown to 154,000 men by 1756. His army was adept at drills and discipline and this paid off. His troops could move into position flawlessly and execute complex tactics. The Prussian infantry carried flintlock muskets with bayonets.

Marching gaiters

This image (left) depicts soldiers in red, yellow and white uniforms. It is from a 1789 publication entitled *Preussische Armee Uniformen unter Friedrich Wilhelm II*, meaning 'Prussian Army Uniforms under Frederick William II'.

A BRAVE LEADER
Frederick twice had his horse shot from under him on the battlefield and was wounded himself. He is pictured below with two of the 5th Hussars (a unit of light cavalry soldiers).

Frederick the Great

Hussar

AMERICAN REVOLUTION, 1775-83

America

Re-creation of a British redcoat

Felt hat

Bayonet

After a series of expensive conflicts in Europe, Britain decided to raise money through increased taxation of its American colonists. The thirteen British colonies on the Eastern seaboard were deeply unhappy about paying these taxes, as they had no representation in the English Parliament.

When the British attempted to seize a large arms cache at Concord in Massachusetts, the Americans attacked. Although the casualties were relatively low, the war and the fight for freedom had begun.

REDCOATS
This British soldier (right) is in full marching uniform, with a knapsack, felt hat and gaiters. He also carries a flintlock rifle with a removable bayonet.

A 'lion's head' sabre, as used by naval officers

Flintlock rifle

Gaiters

THE WAR AT SEA
American privateers caused problems for British trade ships, but did not threaten the British Navy until the French entered the war in 1778. After this, there were many battles in the waters off America (above).

CONTINENTALS

In 1776 George Washington persuaded Congress to raise a Continental regular army. Each state provided soldiers for the force. The soldiers were given a musket, cartridge box, bayonet belt and coat. They had to supply their own shirt, breeches, socks and shoes.

French

Spanish

British

Map of the east side of North America (above) showing how the land was divided between the colonial powers before the Seven Years' War

THE SEVEN YEARS' WAR

Europe had been in turmoil between 1756 and 1763, with Britain and Prussia fighting against France and Austria because of commercial and colonial rivalry (see pages 20-21). There were bitter disputes between Britain and France over territory in North America and this led the French to join the campaign to rid the continent of British rule.

MINUTEMEN

Each American colony had a group of volunteer soldiers called 'minutemen' (below left) as they were expected to be ready to fight at a minute's notice. These soldiers had the words 'Liberty or Death' on their caps and carried their belongings wrapped in a blanket worn as a bandolier.

Musket

Bayonet

Breeches

Minuteman

Continental soldiers

Bandolier

Re-creation of a soldier in Washington's Continental army

BATTLES FOR INDEPENDENCE

*I*n the Autumn of 1775 the Americans invaded Canada in a attempt to cut off the British in New England. After a six-week siege, Fort St. Jean surrendered, as did the forces at Fort Chambly and Montreal. In 1777 the British tried to cut the thirteen colonies in half and won victories at Brandywine and Germantown, but the strategy failed after battles at Bemis Heights and Bennington. With the arrival of the French in 1778, the power balance shifted and the British moved south. The end of the war came with the Battle of Yorktown, Virginia, in 1781 (below). The British force, under General Cornwallis, was surrounded by the forces of Washington (American) and Rochambeau (French). America had finally won its independence.

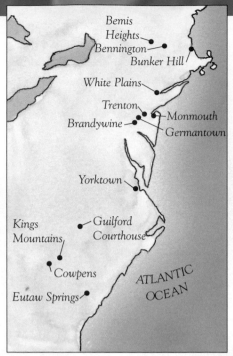

Map (above) showing the major battles of the American War of Independence, from Bunker Hill to the British surrender at Yorktown in 1781

24

An 18th-century oil painting depicting British troops attacking the Americans at the Battle of Bunker Hill

An 18th-century coloured engraving depicting the British surrendering to George Washington after their defeat at Yorktown

BUNKER HILL, 17TH JUNE, 1775

The first major battle of the war took place at Bunker Hill (above). The Americans who were entrenched on top of the hill inflicted heavy casualties on the British lines of infantry. However, with the Americans running out of ammunition, the British eventually drove them back.

BRITISH SURRENDER

Besieged at Yorktown, Cornwallis and the British troops sustained heavy bombardment for 14 days. British ships bringing more troops to relieve Yorktown were blocked at Virginia Capes by the French Navy under Admiral De Grasse. Under constant fire and with no sign of relief, Cornwallis surrendered (above).

Continentals bombarding Yorktown with artillery

NAPOLEONIC WARS, 1797-1815

Napoleon Bonaparte

Napoleon rose out of the chaos of the violent revolution in France (1787-1799), in which the king, queen and thousands of others were executed. Born in Corsica in 1769, the young Bonaparte was sent to French military school and graduated to become a lieutenant in the artillery. In 1796 he took command of the French army in Italy to counter the threat of an Austrian invasion. Within a year he had driven them out. He fought with new tactics, often marching at night, attacking in the rain and even on Sundays (unheard of before). Napoleon next attacked Egypt to disrupt British trade routes. At first he was successful – at the Battle of Cairo on 21st July, 1798 and defeating the Egyptian Mamelukes army at Giza, capturing Suez. However, at the Battle of the Nile on 1st August, 1798, the French fleet was destroyed. They lost six ships (four sunk, two captured) to British Admiral Nelson.

Bearskin helmet

Cartridge box

Flintlock musket

Re-creation of soldiers from the Napoleonic Imperial Guard

SHAKO PLATE
Worn on the front of a soldier's helmet, the shako plate (above) was decorated with the symbol of an eagle and marked with the maxim of the French Republic: 'Liberté, Egalité, Fraternité' (Freedom, Equality, Brotherhood).

Hussar

Polish Lancer

Dragoon

UNIFORMS
The Napoleonic era was a 'golden age' of military uniforms (above and right), which were as grand as possible, both to impress the enemy and to raise the morale of the wearer. Unfortunately, this meant that at times they were not particularly practical.

NELSON'S NAVY

I t has been said that all that separated Britain from an invasion by Napoleon were the ships of the British Navy (nicknamed the 'Wooden Walls'). In 1789 there were around 16,000 officers and men in naval service and by 1803 this had risen to 120,000 due to the war with France. At this time the Navy had over 110 warships which were used to defend the country, attack enemy navies, control distant colonies and protect merchant ships. Britain's strong sea power made her one of the most powerful nations in the world during this period.

NELSON (1758-1805)

Horatio Nelson rose rapidly through the ranks to become a captain at only 21. His bold leadership brought him decisive victories at the Nile (1798) and Copenhagen (1801). His most famous victory at the Battle of Trafalgar (1805) cost him his life.

MEMBERS OF THE CREW

The crew of a ship like the *Victory* was enormous: 600 strong, including 150 marines, as well as 20 officers, lieutenants and the captain.

Captain

Lieutenant

Midshipman (with a speaking trumpet)

'Powder monkey'– a man who supplied the gunners with gunpowder

Horatio Nelson

Gun crews (above) worked quickly on deck. It took an experienced crew two to five minutes to clean, load, aim and fire a cannon.

VARIOUS SHOT

There were different types of projectiles for different purposes: to cut down sails and rigging, to kill enemy soldiers and to penetrate the wooden hulls of enemy ships.

Various types of shot

HMS VICTORY

Nelson's flagship, *HMS Victory* (below), was built between 1759-65 from around 2,000 oak trees. The *Victory* was a 'first rate' ship, meaning she had 100 guns or more. These were distributed along four gun decks on each side of the ship.

HMS Victory

Detail from the HMS Victory

Gun ports

Large ships like the Victory were difficult to handle and she had 32 different sails and about 38 km of rigging.

CROSSING THE LINE

Tactics were to 'cross the line' (right) of enemy fleets to separate them into smaller units and enable all guns to fire at once on a target.

Diagram showing how a ship would 'cross the line'

BATTLE OF TRAFALGAR, 1805

In 1805 Napoleon planned to invade Britain. He ordered Admiral Villeneuve's combined Franco-Spanish fleet to make a diversionary voyage, before returning to cover the invasion. Nelson chased this fleet back to Spain and the invasion plan was abandoned. The Franco-Spanish fleet then sailed to support French forces in the Mediterranean. Nelson's  fleet of 27 ships intercepted it at Cape Trafalgar (off the Spanish coast) on 21st October and after an epic sea battle (above) 19 of Napoleon's 33 ships surrendered or were destroyed.

PENINSULAR WARS

*I*n 1804 Napoleon appointed himself emperor of France. In the following years he had great military successes, first against the Russians and Austrians at Austerlitz and later against the Prussians in a series of lightning attacks. In 1807 Napoleon decided to enforce a blockade of British trade by invading Spain and Portugal, where he installed his cousin Joseph Bonaparte as king. British General Sir Arthur Wellesly landed a small army in Portugal to drive the French out and the Peninsular Wars began. Although he won initial battles at Rolica and Vimiero, the British were forced to retreat to Corunna for the winter. Wellesly then advanced rapidly and drove the French out of Portugal. In 1810 the French, under Marshal Massena, invaded Spain and Portugal once more, but were defeated at Fuentes d'Onoro (1811) and Salamanca (1812). After five years of bloody conflict, the Peninsular Wars ended in 1813, when the French evacuated Madrid. It was a sign that French domination of Europe was coming to an end.

Map showing the Spanish peninsula and the major battles of the campaign

THE BATTLE OF SALAMANCA
This was a decisive blow to Napoleon's grip on the Spanish peninsula. More than 7,000 French troops were killed and a further 7,000 were captured, when they tried to attack the Duke of Wellington's army near Salamanca (below).

Captured French troops being led into Salamanca (below)

A flintlock pistol from the Napoleonic era

As well as a sabre, French cavalry troops would have carried a pistol (above)

Peaked helmet ——

Curved sword ——

Decorative tassles in the hussar style ——

ARTHUR WELLESLY, DUKE OF WELLINGTON

Known as 'The Iron Duke' by his soldiers, Wellesly (above) was born in Ireland and joined the British army in 1787. In 1796 he was posted to India and became a prominent soldier and administrator and on his return to Britain was knighted. He took command of the British forces against Napoleon in the Peninsular Wars and was made Duke of Wellington in 1814.

CAVALRY

Troops on horseback were divided into heavy and light units. Heavy cavalry were used for shock tactics and would try to smash through the enemy line by brute force. The light cavalry (right), used mostly for flanking maneouvres and pursuit, wore no armour and carried curved swords for slashing. Massed for the attack, they were an imposing sight. Walking slowly towards the enemy's troops, they patiently waited for the signal to charge as shot and shells rained down on them.

Re-creation of a member of the British light cavalry

ROAD TO WATERLOO

In 1813 Austria and Prussia rose up to fight the French. While Napoleon managed to defend his territory in Germany, Wellington advanced through Spain and entered France from the south in the spring of 1814. While Napoleon tried to resist an invasion from the eastern allies, Paris fell to an allied coalition and he was forced to give up the throne and go into exile on the island of Elba. However, in March 1815 he escaped and returned to France, where he still had the support of his old guard. On 16th June he made a sudden advance into Belgium and defeated the Prussian General Blucher at the Battle of Ligny. Napoleon's final stand was on 18th June, when he met Wellington's army at Waterloo in Belgium. With Prussian help, Wellington defeated Napoleon and the once-great military commander went into exile for good on the island of St Helena.

FIRING A BROWN BESS FLINTLOCK

a) Take a cartridge from side pouch and bite off the end.
b) Pour a small amount of power on the priming pan.
c) Put the ball and paper down the muzzle of the musket.
d) Use the ramrod to push the ball down to the end of the barrel.
e) Pull the cock back with thumb. This has the striking flint in it.
f) Take aim.
g) Fire!

THE BROWN BESS FLINTLOCK

This smoothbore, muzzle-loading, flintlock musket was used by British troops in the Napoleonic Wars. Well-trained infantry could fire three rounds a minute, an incredible rate considering the number of stages required to load the weapon. Although its effective range was roughly 135 m, British troops normally held their fire until the enemy were as close as 50 m. At this distance a volley of fire would be deadly.

Brown Bess
flintlock musket

BRITISH INFANTRY REDCOAT

Most young men joined the army for the money and few for adventure and glory. They weren't paid particularly well – a shilling a day, of which nine pence was kept for expenses – but if you were a penniless labourer this was much better than starving.

Re-creation of a British infantry redcoat from the Napoleonic era

Blanket

Musket

Ration bag

Cartridge box

BRITISH BATTLE FORMATIONS

The 'square' was the best formation for defence against cavalry attack. Soldiers would line up on each side of a square in four ranks. This meant that two ranks could fire while two were reloading. The officers and the company flags were in the centre. Another tactic, the 'thin red line', consisted of two ranks of infantry used to fire at three sides of an attacking column of infantry.

The 'thin red line'

Infantry

Enemy infantry

The 'square'

Infantry ranks

Officers and flags

CRIMEAN WAR, 1854-56

When Russia marched into Ottoman territories across the River Danube in March 1854, both Britain and France grew concerned. Britain was fearful that Russia would threaten British trade with India and the new leader of France, Napoleon III, was worried about French interests in the area. So, on 28th March, 1854, Britain and France declared war on Russia. The allied forces, led by Lord Ragland (British) and Marshal St. Arnaud (French), reached the Black Sea in August, 1854. On 14th September the allies landed at Eupatoria on the Crimean coast. The inferior Russian forces were defeated at Alma River on 20th September, Balaclava on 25th October and Inkerman on 5th November and, after a year-long siege, the Russian naval base at Sevastopol surrendered to the allies on 10th September, 1855. The new Russian Tsar Alexander II signed a surrender in Paris on 30th March, 1856, ending the war and securing the neutrality of the Black Sea.

CHARGE OF THE LIGHT BRIGADE
The Charge of the Light Brigade (below) at Balaclava was one of Britain's most notorious military actions. As a result of confusion over orders a brigade of light cavalry were ordered to charge down a narrow valley 2.5 km long, straight at thirty Russian cannon as well as batteries on either side. One of the cavalry regiments was the 17th Lancers (below).

A bugle used in the charge
of the Light Brigade

HOSPITALS

Medical conditions for men injured in battle were appalling. After reports of the terrible sanitation in a hospital in Scutari, Turkey, appeared in the newspapers, a woman called Florence Nightingale  (left) obtained permission to take nurses to the Crimea to clean up the hospital. When she arrived on 7th November, 1854, doctors refused to help her until they were overloaded with wounded from the Battle of Inkerman. At that time, up to 42 per cent of casualties admitted died in the rat-infested hospital. With Nightingale's strict regime of cleanliness and the nurses' efforts, this was cut to 2 per cent.

Map showing the major battles of
the Crimean War (above)

Shako helmet

Lance

Blue double-
breasted uniform

Cartridge box

A MASSACRE

Of the 607 brigadiers who rode out in the Charge of the Light Brigade, only 198 returned. Although the brave and foolhardy charge had no military value, the British won the battle against a much stronger Russian force.

Re-creation of a member
of the Light Brigade

America

AMERICAN CIVIL WAR

From 1861 to 1865 America was torn apart by a civil war between northern (Union) and southern (Confederate) states. The conflict arose over laws imposed on the southern states by the national government of President Lincoln. Some individual states wanted to govern themselves. Thirty years of quarrels over issues including trade and slavery finally erupted into war. It was the first major conflict to make use of 19th-century technology: generals communicated with each other by telegraph; balloons were used to spy on enemy positions; ironclads started to replace wooden ships; troops and supplies were moved by trains.

In the late stages of the war, the armies dug in and trench warfare developed. Barbed wire and early machine guns were used on the battlefield. Around 600,000 people died, making it the bloodiest war in the history of America. It could be said the Civil War was the first 'modern' war and an indicator of the carnage to come in the First World War.

Bayonet scabbard

Musket

Re-creation of a soldier in the Union army

A UNION SOLDIER
For the wealthier Union army, uniforms were standard – a dark blue jacket and sky-blue trousers. Equipment included a knapsack, a rolled blanket, a cartridge box, a water-bottle and a rifle fixed with a bayonet. Muskets now had spiral grooves, or rifling, which made a musket ball spin. This gave the weapon a longer range and better accuracy.

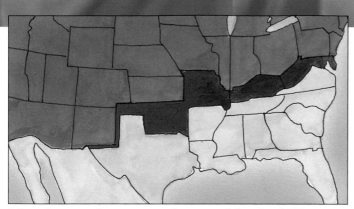

Map showing America on the eve of the Civil War

- ■ Union states
- ▨ Confederate states
- ■ States which later joined the Confederacy

The southern Confederate states were Alabama, Mississippi, Arkansas, Georgia, Tennessee, Virginia, Texas, Louisiana, Florida and North and South Carolina. Nebraska and Kansas were bought from France in the 1803 Louisiana Purchase. In 1836 Texas won its independence from Mexico and became a state in 1845. California and New Mexico were gained in the Mexican War of 1848.

A pistol with attached bayonet for close combat

PISTOLS

At the beginning of the war, neither army had an official pistol, but by the end, pistols were being manufactured in their thousands.

REPEATING RIFLES

The Spencer carbine was issued to Union troops in late 1863 as a cavalry firearm. The gun was both superbly crafted and highly accurate. With its seven-round capacity, this proved to be a very effective weapon for firing on horseback. It was nicknamed 'Spencer and his seven devils'.

A CONFEDERATE SOLDIER

The poorer Confederate army had little means of manufacturing clothing. They wore grey and brown makeshift uniforms (right). In the later stages of the war they often used parts of captured Union uniforms and weapons. A Confederate carried a knapsack, a cartridge box, a wooden water-bottle and a rifle with a bayonet. Across his shoulder was a blanket roll. He often kept a tin pot for making coffee. Infantrymen used long muskets but cavalry units on both sides favoured the shorter carbine.

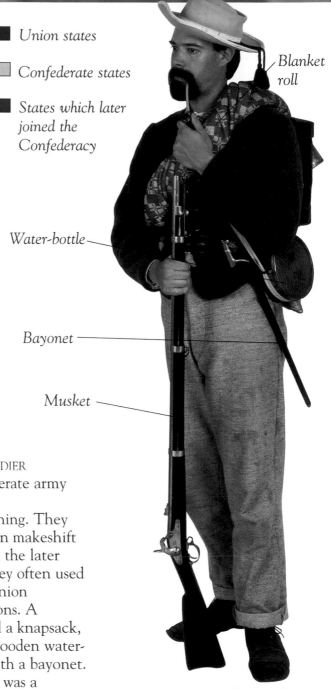

- Blanket roll
- Water-bottle
- Bayonet
- Musket

Re-creation of a soldier in the Confederate army

Butt of a Spencer carbine rifle

THE UNION VICTORY

The first major battle of the American Civil War showed that there would be no easy victory for the Union troops. They were driven back when they tried to break through Confederate lines at Bull Run, Virginia. However, later in the war, their superior numbers and equipment began to tell. Though the Confederates repeatedly attempted to rally and fight back, they spent a great deal of time in retreat. In the Battle of Gettysburg in July 1863, they suffered casualties from which they never fully recovered. The Confederate commander, General Lee, was forced to surrender his last 7,800 troops on 9th April, 1865, at Appomattox in Virginia.

ULYSSES S. GRANT
Grant (1822-85), seated third from left in the photo above, entered the war as a colonel of volunteers in support of the Union and was rapidly promoted. He later became the President of the USA from 1867-1877.

ARTILLERY
The war saw a progressive transition from smooth-bore to rifled field guns by both sides.

GUNSHIPS
Floating mortar vessels had no engines, but could heavily bombard enemy positions on land.

TRAINS
The Union used trains to give them an advantage in moving men, supplies and artillery to where they were needed.

IRONCLADS
These new, heavily-armoured warships were almost indestructible. When the *Merrimac* (Confederate) and the *Monitor* (Union) met in battle on 9th March, 1862, the battle raged for four hours before being called off, because the men were exhausted from loading the cannon.

The Union army attacking at Gettysburg

ROBERT E. LEE
Lee (1807-70, left) was the leading Confederate general. He became military advisor to the President of the Southern Confederacy, Jefferson Davis. In 1862 he commanded the Northern Army in victories at Fredericksburg and Chancellorsville. He was a great commander with the resources available to him and sometimes defeated larger Union armies with his superior tactics.

AMERICAN INDIAN WARS, 1854-90

A colt revolver as used in the 'Wild West'

In the mid 1800s a great stream of pioneers, ranchers and gold panners poured into the 'Wild West'. They brought diseases like smallpox which wiped out whole tribes of Native Americans. White hunters slaughtered millions of buffalo and farmers fenced off the huge open plains. One by one the tribes were forced off their land and onto reservations by the US government. Most went peacefully, but others chose to fight – their most famous victory was at the Battle of the Little Big Horn. But the Native American tribes could never entirely defeat the larger and more powerful US army. The soldiers burnt their villages and showed no mercy. By 1890 no Plains Indians remained free.

GENERAL GEORGE CUSTER
Called 'Long Hair' by the Indians, Custer (above) was in command of the 7th Cavalry. He had served in the Civil War on the Union side. He attacked Chief Sitting Bull's huge camp at the Little Big Horn in 1876, but Custer's men were defeated and all 265 were killed.

General

Captain

Cavalryman   Native American scout

INSIDE A FORT
Each captain was in charge of a company of 25 men. A sergeant kept discipline and gave orders day-to-day. Senior officers such as generals and colonels would visit the fort to pass on government orders, negotiate treaties with the Indians or organise attacks on them. Cavalrymen carried sabres, revolvers and rifles. Native American scouts were used to find camps or guide soldiers along trails.

FORT LARAMIE
Fort Laramie (right), Wyoming, was a post thriving with trappers, miners, Native Americans and pioneers on their way westwards. Later, during the Indian Wars, the US army built forts all over the West and Fort Laramie became a military complex.

*Re-creation of a
Native American fighter*

War paint

Bone
breastplate

Rifle and case

Moccasins

Bow

Shield

NATIVE WARRIORS

Native American warriors, like this Cheyenne (left), fought on horseback. They wore war paint to make themselves look fierce. Their weapons cases for guns and bows had decorative bead work, as did their moccasins. They wore a breastplate made out of bone and carried a shield to protect themselves.

SITTING BULL

A warrior and medicine man, Sitting Bull was the most famous of all the Sioux Indians. Along with other chiefs he led his warriors in the war against men who were trying to drive them into reservations. After Little Big Horn he fled to Canada but eventually surrendered.

NATIVE AMERICAN TACTICS

The tribes often used hit-and-run tactics (below), avoiding open battles where they would be out-gunned. They often laid ambushes, drawing soldiers into a trap by using a small group of warriors as bait.

*Native American
rider's gauntlets*

TIMESPAN

American War of Independence

1550-1650
Warring feudal nobles with samurai armies fight over territories in Japan.

1587
Francis Drake makes an expedition to Cadiz and destroys 33 Spanish ships.

English warship

1588
The Spanish Armada attacks England and is repelled by English ships.

1642-46
The English Civil War. King Charles I is beheaded in 1649.

1652
Following the *Navigations Act* (1651) England and the Dutch are at war over control of sea routes and regulation of colonial trade.

1658
At the Battle of the Dunes an Anglo-French alliance defeats the Spanish army.

1688
The 'Glorious Revolution' in Britain. King James II is overthrown and William of Orange is crowned King of Britain. In 1690, at the Battle of the Boyne, James is defeated in Ireland by William III (formerly William of Orange).

1701-14
The War of the Spanish Succession. In the Battle of Blenheim (1704) the British and Prince Eugene of Savoy destroy a Franco-Bavarian force. In 1708, they defeat the French at Oudenarde.

1701
The Kingdom of Prussia is established.

1707
Scotland is formally joined with England and Wales to form the United Kingdom.

1745
The Jacobite rebellion. Bonnie Prince Charlie enters a conflict with George I over the right to the British throne. At the Battle of Culloden in 1746, the Scots are defeated.

1756-63
The Seven Years' War was fought between Russia, Austria and France against the expansion of Prussian power. Frederick II of Prussia defeats the Austrians at Prague in 1757. At the Battle of Zorndorf (1758), Frederick wins and ends the Russian threat. He is defeated by a Austro-Russian force at Kunersdorf in 1759. In 1763, the Treaty of Hubertusburg ends the Seven Years' War, after Tsar Peter III of Russia begins peace talks.

1761-62
The Spanish try to invade Portugal but are driven back.

1775-1783
The American War of Independence. The first shots are fired at Lexington. George Washington takes command of the Continental Army.
After a siege the British abandon Boston. France and Spain give support to the American side. The Battle of Bemis Heights, Saratoga is an American victory and the turning point in the war. In 1781 the Americans besiege Yorktown and British General Cornwallis surrenders.

1782
Britain signs the Treaty of Paris and recognises the independence of the USA.

1797-1815
The Napoleonic Wars. French Emperor Napoleon's Egyptian expedition defeats the Egyptian Mamelukes at Cairo and the French fleet is almost destroyed by Nelson.

1800
Napoleon crosses the Alps into Italy.

1805
British Admiral Nelson wins at the Battle of Trafalgar but loses

Battle of Trafalgar

his life to a French sniper. Napoleon wins battles at Ulm and Austerlitz.

1806
Napoleon wins at Jena, enters Berlin and carries on to Warsaw.

1808
Napoleon starts his Spanish campaign.

1809
The French win the Battle of Wagram against the Austrians.

1812-13
Napoleon attacks Russia and marches to Moscow to find the city in flames. He retreats and his army lose more than 300,000 men in the winter conditions.

1814
While Napoleon resists invasion by Russia, Austria and Prussia, the British Duke of Wellington advances into France from Spain and takes Toulouse. Meanwhile Paris is taken by the eastern allies. Napoleon goes into exile on the island of Elba.

Napoleon Bonaparte

1815
Napoleon escapes from Elba and returns to France. He meets Wellington's army at Waterloo and is defeated after the late arrival of the Prussians.

1854-56
The Crimean War. The French, the British and Ottoman Turks fight against the Russian invasion of Turkish-controlled Christian holy land.

1854
Allied forces defeat the Russians at Alma, Balaclava and Inkerman.

1855
France and Britain capture Sevastopol after a year-long siege.

1856
Peace treaty signed at Paris ends the Crimean War.

1861
The American Civil War begins. Confederates shell Union-held Fort Sumter in South Carolina. Union forces advance on the southern capital, Richmond.

1863
Confederate General Lee loses the Battle at Gettysburg with 31,000 casualties.

1864
Union General Grant invades the South with a larger and better equipped army. Lee's Northern Army is pinned down defending Petersburg and Richmond.

1865
On 9th April, General Lee is forced to surrender at

Appomattox, Virginia, ending the war. On 14th April President Lincoln is assassinated.

1854
The American Indian Wars begin.

1862
Little Crow the Younger leads a Sioux uprising.

1870
The Franco-Prussian War lasts 44 days. Napoleon III of France surrenders on 2nd September at Sedan to Kaiser William.

1874
Colonel Mackenzie defeats the Comanches at Red River.

1876
Chief Sitting Bull unifies the Sioux and defeats General Custer at the Battle of the Little Big Horn.

American Indian Wars

1877
The famous Native warrior Crazy Horse is killed at Fort Robinson, Nebraska.

1889
Geronimo surrenders.

1890
The Battle of Wounded Knee – the final battle of the American Indian Wars.

GLOSSARY

Armada A large number of ships.

Artillery High calibre guns.

Bandolier A soldier's shoulder belt with small pockets or loops for gun cartridges.

Battery An artillery unit.

Bayonet A blade attached to a gun for close-combat fighting.

Cache A store of weapons.

Cartridges Ammunition for firearms.

Casualty A soldier killed or wounded in enemy action.

Cavalier A supporter of King Charles I during the English Civil War.

Cavalry Troops who fight on horseback.

Clan A group of families with a common ancestor.

Colony A territory occupied and ruled by a foreign state.

Confederacy The southern states which fought the Union army in the American Civil War.

Continental The name given to the British who fought to keep 13 northern states in the American War of Independence.

Drill Training in military procedures.

Empire Territory under the rule of a sovereign state.

Exile A forced absence from one's home or country.

Expansionism The policy of expanding the territory of a country.

Gold panner Someone searching for gold.

Grenade An explosive thrown by hand.

Infantry Soldiers who fight on foot.

Ironclad A warship with iron plating.

Jacobite A Scottish follower of James II.

Moccasins Soft leather shoes.

Morale The spirit of optimism within a group or individual.

Ottoman Empire The Turkish empire.

Privateer A privately owned ship authorised by government.

Redcoat A type of British soldier.

Reservation An area of land set aside for American Indians.

Revolver A pistol with a cylindrical chamber for bullets.

Roundhead A supporter of

Parliament during the English Civil War.

Royalist A supporter of the ruling monarch.

Sabre A type of sword with a curved blade.

Samurai A Japanese warrior.

Shogun A Japanese military commander.

Smallpox A highly contagious disease.

Sniper A concealed rifleman.

Speaking trumpet An instrument that makes the speaker's voice louder.

Succession When a nation passes from one leader to another.

Tactics Military maneouvres to outwit an enemy.

Taxes A compulsory payment to the government.

Treaty An agreement between nations or states.

Uniform Clothes which show which side a soldier belongs to.

Union The northern states in the American Civil War.

Volunteer A person who serves their country willingly.

INDEX

Page numbers in **bold** refer to illustrations.